THE SEVEN VALLEYS
AND
THE FOUR VALLEYS

The Seven Valleys and the Four Valleys

Bahá'u'lláh

Translated by MARZIEH GAIL
In consultation with ALI-KULI KHAN

BAHÁ'Í PUBLISHING TRUST
Wilmette, Illinois

Library of Congress Cataloging in Publication Data

Bahá Ulláh, 1817-1892
  The seven valleys and The four valleys.

  Translation of Haft vádí and Chahár vádí.
  Includes bibliographical references.
  1. Bahaism. I. Bahá Ulláh, 1817-1892. Chahár vádí.
English. 1977. II. Title.
BP360.B6313   1977   297'.892   77-23326
ISBN 0-87743-113-2
ISBN 0-87743-114-0 pbk.

CONTENTS

Seven Valleys and Four Valleys should be regarded as independent Tablets, as they were revealed to different persons.

—SHOGHI EFFENDI

PREFACE

The Bahá'í Faith came into being in Shíráz, Persia, the night of May 22, 1844. 'Alí Muḥammad, a descendant of Muḥammad, stunned His young guest, Mullá Ḥusayn, by declaring Himself to be a Messenger of God. He assumed the title of Báb or Gate. Like John the Baptist, He claimed to be the Herald of One greater than Himself. Beyond this, He claimed to be an independent Prophet with authority to change existing religious practices and to reveal prayers and laws. His message would be supplanted by that of "Him Whom God shall manifest."

The Báb was born in Shíráz, Persia, the city of the poets Ḥáfiẓ and Sa'dí, on October 20, 1819. When He was a child, His goodness and innate knowledge amazed His teacher. Later, His sense of probity and justice as a merchant set a standard for the business community.

The years following the Báb's Declaration were filled with turmoil. In a single year, the ferociously fanatical and ignorant Persian Muslims murdered 4,000 adherents of His Cause. The first to believe in Him was shot from ambush; His greatest disciple, Quddús, was torn to pieces in the public square of Bárfurús̲h̲ (Bábul). Ṭáhirih, the most outstanding Bábí woman, bravely and defiantly cried out to her captors, "You can kill me as soon as you like but you cannot stop the emancipation of women."

Among the Báb's many books, some written while a prisoner in the mountains of Ád̲h̲irbáyján, the most widely known are the Persian *Bayán* and the Arabic *Bayán*. These works were translated into French by A. L. M. Nicolas, the Persian-born French consul at Tabríz who was fascinated by the life and teachings of the Prophet of S̲h̲íráz.

It was for the love of Bahá'u'lláh, the Glory of God, that the Báb sacrificed His life. His dramatic martyrdom took place in the windswept barracks square of Tabríz at noon on July 9, 1850.

2.

The central figure in the second period of Bahá'í history was Bahá'u'lláh, the One foretold by the Báb. He was born in Ṭihrán, Persia, on November 12, 1817. His given name was Ḥusayn 'Alí; later He assumed the title Bahá'u'lláh, meaning "Glory of God."

Ḥusayn 'Alí was of a noble, respected, and wealthy family. A career in government service was open to Him, but He was not interested in politics. His kingdom was not of this world. Turning His back on a life of luxury, He early championed the Cause of the Báb. He knew that this action would lead to privation, suffering, and persecution for Himself and His loved ones. The blow fell in August 1852 when He was incarcerated in the Black Pit of the capital of Persia. In this underground dungeon, He was surrounded by thieves and murderers. Heavy chains and fetters cut into His flesh. Amidst the horror, agony, and gloom of this place, the Revelation of Bahá'u'lláh was born. The "Most Great Spirit" appeared to Him in a dream, and on every side were heard these words: *"Verily, we shall render Thee victorious by Thyself and by Thy pen. Grieve Thou not for that which hath befallen Thee, neither be Thou afraid, for Thou art in safety. Erelong will God raise up the treasures of the earth—men who will aid Thee through Thyself and through Thy name, wherewith God hath revived the hearts of such as have recognized Him."*

In January 1853, Bahá'u'lláh and His family were banished from Persia. He chose Baghdád as the place of exile. The midwinter journey followed a tortuous route through the icy mountains of Kirmánsháh westward to the city astride the Tigris. As the years went by, the popularity of Bahá'u'lláh grew, and leaders of thought would gather informally around Him along the riverside and seek His views.

He would walk along the Tigris, sometimes resting at a mosque that remains as a witness of those days, and compose *The Hidden Words*, lovely verses that sum up the essentials of religion. His foremost work in Baghdád was *The Book of Certitude*. This dealt with the theme of progressive revelation, the doctrine that Prophets reveal teachings according to the needs and capacity of the people. His influence waxed too strong to suit the rulers of Persia and Turkey, and they decided to send Him farther from His homeland.

On April 22, 1863, He left His home, crossed the Tigris, and pitched His tent in a garden which He named the Garden of Riḍván or Paradise. Here He declared to His trusted friends that He was the Manifestation of God, sent to earth to bring the long-promised reign of righteousness.

Exile followed in Constantinople and in Adrianople, where Bahá'u'lláh publicly proclaimed His mission. In Adrianople in 1863, He revealed the Tablet of the Kings (Súriy-i-Mulúk), warning the kings of East and West that disobedience to God would lead to their downfall.

Bahá'u'lláh was finally exiled in 1868 to the ancient prison at 'Akká, Palestine, the St. Jean d'Acre of the Crusaders. In the Holy Land, He wrote the Kitáb-i-Aqdas, or Most Holy Book. In it He prescribes obligatory prayers, sets the dates for fasting and festivals, and condemns backbiting, idleness, and cruelty to animals. The book forbids the use of opium and alcohol for other than scientific purposes and prohibits slavery, begging, and monasticism. It ordains monogamy and interdicts gambling. The writing of a testament is held to be a duty. Every Bahá'í is commanded to obey his government. Among the Bahá'í virtures are spotless cleanliness, chastity, trustworthiness, hospitality, courtesy, and justice.

3.

The Seven Valleys of Bahá'u'lláh may be regarded as the summit of achievement in the realm of mystical composition. This profound essay was written in response to questions of Shaykh Muḥyi'd-Dín, the judge of Khániqín, a town situated near the Persian border northeast of Baghdád. The judge was evidently a student of Ṣúfí philosophy, a variety of mysticism that developed as a movement within Islám. The goal of the Ṣúfí was to attain the Presence of God through meditation and prayer, contemplation and ecstacy. A special terminology was developed to explain the stages of spiritual progress. Some Ṣúfís embraced the doctrine that they could approach God directly without assistance from Muḥammad or other Prophets. This view logically led to the tenet that the Ṣúfís were exempt from the laws of religion and that for them, even if not for the multitude, conscience was a safe guide. The greatest of the Persian mystics, Jalálu'd-Dín Rúmí and al-Ghazzálí, contested this theory, affirming that only through obedience to the laws of God as revealed by His Messengers could one attain unto the Divine Presence.

Shaykh Muḥyi'd-Dín was doubtless conversant with the writings of the twelfth century Persian Ṣúfí, Farídu'd-Dín 'Aṭṭár. 'Aṭṭár's most esteemed work was the *Mantiqu'ṭ-Ṭayr* or Language of the Birds. In it the journey of the soul is traced through Seven Valleys: Search, Love, Knowledge, Detachment, Unification, Bewilderment, and Annihilation. Bahá'u'lláh employed a similar, although not identical, pattern in His Persian *Seven Valleys* which delineates the seven stages of progress of the soul toward the object of its being. Bahá'u'lláh wrote this work after His return to Baghdád from the mountains near Sulaymáníyyih. The subject is essentially timeless and placeless, the inner verities of religion. The spiritual realities are the same in all the established religions, and they constitute the foundation of faith. This is the purport of the declaration of Bahá'u'lláh concerning His Faith: "This is the changeless Faith of God, eternal in the past, eternal in the future."

The *Four Valleys,* an epistle written in Baghdád

after the composition of the *Seven Valleys,* was addressed to the learned S̲h̲ayk̲h̲ 'Abdu'r-Raḥmán of Karkúk, a city of 'Iráqí Kurdistán. It sets forth four ways in which the Unseen is seen, the four stages of the human heart, and the four kinds of mystic wayfarers in quest of the Intended One, the Praiseworthy One, the Attracting One, the Beloved. The four divine states are given in this verse from the Qur'án (57:3): "He is the first and the last; the Seen and the Hidden; and He knoweth all things."

—ROBERT L. GULICK, JR.
February 1, 1975

xiii

THE SEVEN VALLEYS

of

BAHÁ'U'LLÁH

In the Name of God, the Clement, the Merciful.

Praise be to God Who hath made being to come forth from nothingness; graven upon the tablet of man the mysteries of preexistence; taught him from the Bayán that which he knew not; made him a Luminous Book unto those who believed and surrendered themselves; caused him to witness the creation of all things (Kullu Shay') in this black and ruinous age, and to speak forth from the apex of eternity with a wondrous voice in the Excellent Temple[1]: to the end that every man may testify, in himself, by himself, in the station of the Manifestation of his Lord, that verily there is no God save Him, and that every man may thereby win his way to the

1. The Manifestation.

I

summit of realities, until none shall contemplate anything whatsoever but that he shall see God therein.

And I praise and glorify the first sea which hath branched from the ocean of the Divine Essence, and the first morn which hath glowed from the Horizon of Oneness, and the first sun which hath risen in the Heaven of Eternity, and the first fire which was lit from the Lamp of Preexistence in the lantern of singleness: He who was Aḥmad in the kingdom of the exalted ones, and Muḥammad amongst the concourse of the near ones, and Maḥmúd[2] in the realm of the sincere ones. ". . . by whichsoever (name) ye will, invoke Him: He hath most excellent names"[3] in the hearts of those who know. And upon His household and companions be abundant and abiding and eternal peace!

Further, we have harkened to what the nightingale of knowledge sang on the boughs of the tree of thy being, and learned what the dove of certitude cried on the branches of the bower of thy heart. Methinks I verily inhaled the pure fragrances of the garment of thy love, and

2. Muḥammad, Aḥmad and Maḥmúd are names and titles of the Prophet, derived from the verb "to praise," "to exalt."

3. Qur'án 17:110.

2

attained thy very meeting from perusing thy letter. And since I noted thy mention of thy death in God, and thy life through Him, and thy love for the beloved of God and the Manifestations of His Names and the Dawning-Points of His Attributes—I therefore reveal unto thee sacred and resplendent tokens from the planes of glory, to attract thee into the court of holiness and nearness and beauty, and draw thee to a station wherein thou shalt see nothing in creation save the Face of thy Beloved One, the Honored, and behold all created things only as in the day wherein none hath a mention.

Of this hath the nightingale of oneness sung in the garden of Ghawthíyyih.[4] He saith: "And there shall appear upon the tablet of thine heart a writing of the subtle mysteries of 'Fear God and God will give you knowledge';[5] and the bird of thy soul shall recall the holy sanctuaries of preexistence and soar on the wings of longing in the heaven of 'walk the beaten paths of thy Lord',[6] and gather the fruits of communion in the gardens of 'Then feed on every kind of fruit.' "[6]

By My life, O friend, wert thou to taste of these fruits, from the green garden of these

4. Sermon by 'Alí.   6. Qur'án 16:71.
5. Qur'án 2:282.

3

blossoms which grow in the lands of knowledge, beside the orient lights of the Essence in the mirrors of names and attributes—yearning would seize the reins of patience and reserve from out thy hand, and make thy soul to shake with the flashing light, and draw thee from the earthly homeland to the first, heavenly abode in the Center of Realities, and lift thee to a plane wherein thou wouldst soar in the air even as thou walkest upon the earth, and move over the water as thou runnest on the land. Wherefore, may it rejoice Me, and thee, and whosoever mounteth into the heaven of knowledge, and whose heart is refreshed by this, that the wind of certitude hath blown over the garden of his being, from the Sheba of the All-Merciful.

Peace be upon him who followeth the Right Path!

And further: The stages that mark the wayfarer's journey from the abode of dust to the heavenly homeland are said to be seven. Some have called these Seven Valleys, and others, Seven Cities. And they say that until the wayfarer taketh leave of self, and traverseth these stages, he shall never reach to the ocean of nearness and union, nor drink of the peerless wine. The first is

4

THE VALLEY OF SEARCH

The steed of this Valley is patience; without patience the wayfarer on this journey will reach nowhere and attain no goal. Nor should he ever be downhearted; if he strive for a hundred thousand years and yet fail to behold the beauty of the Friend, he should not falter. For those who seek the Ka'bih[7] of "for Us" rejoice in the tidings: "In Our ways will We guide them."[8] In their search, they have stoutly girded up the loins of service, and seek at every moment to journey from the plane of heedlessness into the realm of being. No bond shall hold them back, and no counsel shall deter them.

It is incumbent on these servants that they cleanse the heart—which is the wellspring of divine treasures—from every marking, and that they turn away from imitation, which is following the traces of their forefathers and sires, and shut the door of friendliness and enmity upon all the people of the earth.

In this journey the seeker reacheth a stage wherein he seeth all created things wandering

---

7. The holy Sanctuary at Mecca. Here the word means "goal."

8. Qur'án 29:69: "And whoso maketh efforts for Us, in Our ways will We guide them."

distracted in search of the Friend. How many a Jacob will he see, hunting after his Joseph; he will behold many a lover, hasting to seek the Beloved, he will witness a world of desiring ones searching after the One Desired. At every moment he findeth a weighty matter, in every hour he becometh aware of a mystery; for he hath taken his heart away from both worlds, and set out for the Ka'bih[7] of the Beloved. At every step, aid from the Invisible Realm will attend him and the heat of his search will grow.

One must judge of search by the standard of the Majnún of Love.[9] It is related that one day they came upon Majnún sifting the dust, and his tears flowing down. They said, "What doest thou?" He said, "I seek for Laylí." They cried, "Alas for thee! Laylí is of pure spirit, and thou seekest her in the dust!" He said, "I seek her everywhere; haply somewhere I shall find her."

Yea, although to the wise it be shameful to

9. Literally, Majnún means "insane." This is the title of the celebrated lover of ancient Persian and Arabian lore, whose beloved was Laylí, daughter of an Arabian prince. Symbolizing true human love bordering on the divine, the story has been made the theme of many a Persian romantic poem, particularly that of Niẓámí, written in 1188-1189 A.D.

6

seek the Lord of Lords in the dust, yet this betokeneth intense ardor in searching. "Whoso seeketh out a thing with zeal shall find it."[10]

The true seeker hunteth naught but the object of his quest, and the lover hath no desire save union with his beloved. Nor shall the seeker reach his goal unless he sacrifice all things. That is, whatever he hath seen, and heard, and understood, all must he set at naught, that he may enter the realm of the spirit, which is the City of God. Labor is needed, if we are to seek Him; ardor is needed, if we are to drink of the honey of reunion with Him; and if we taste of this cup, we shall cast away the world.

On this journey the traveler abideth in every land and dwelleth in every region. In every face, he seeketh the beauty of the Friend; in every country he looketh for the Beloved. He joineth every company, and seeketh fellowship with every soul, that haply in some mind he may uncover the secret of the Friend, or in some face he may behold the beauty of the Loved One.

And if, by the help of God, he findeth on this journey a trace of the traceless Friend, and inhaleth the fragrance of the long-lost Joseph

10. Arabian proverb.

7

from the heavenly messenger,[11] he shall straightway step into

THE VALLEY OF LOVE

and be dissolved in the fire of love. In this city the heaven of ecstasy is upraised and the world-illuming sun of yearning shineth, and the fire of love is ablaze; and when the fire of love is ablaze, it burneth to ashes the harvest of reason.

Now is the traveler unaware of himself, and of aught besides himself. He seeth neither ignorance nor knowledge, neither doubt nor certitude; he knoweth not the morn of guidance from the night of error. He fleeth both from unbelief and faith, and deadly poison is a balm to him. Wherefore 'Aṭṭár[12] saith:

For the infidel, error—for the faithful, faith;
For 'Aṭṭár's heart, an atom of Thy pain.

The steed of this Valley is pain; and if there be no pain this journey will never end. In this station the lover hath no thought save the Beloved, and seeketh no refuge save the Friend.

11. Refer to the story of Joseph in the Qur'án and the Old Testament.

12. Farídu'd-Dín 'Aṭṭár (ca. 1150-1230 A.D.), the great Persian Ṣúfí poet.

At every moment he offereth a hundred lives in the path of the Loved One, at every step he throweth a thousand heads at the feet of the Beloved.

O My Brother! Until thou enter the Egypt of love, thou shalt never come to the Joseph of the Beauty of the Friend; and until, like Jacob, thou forsake thine outward eyes, thou shalt never open the eye of thine inward being; and until thou burn with the fire of love, thou shalt never commune with the Lover of Longing.

A lover feareth nothing and no harm can come nigh him: Thou seest him chill in the fire and dry in the sea.

A lover is he who is chill in hell fire;
A knower is he who is dry in the sea.[13]

Love accepteth no existence and wisheth no life: He seeth life in death, and in shame seeketh glory. To merit the madness of love, man must abound in sanity; to merit the bonds of the Friend, he must be full of spirit. Blessed the neck that is caught in His noose, happy the head that falleth on the dust in the pathway of His love. Wherefore, O friend, give up thy self that thou mayest find the Peerless One, pass by this mortal earth that thou mayest seek

13. Persian mystic poem.

a home in the nest of heaven. Be as naught, if thou wouldst kindle the fire of being and be fit for the pathway of love.

Love seizeth not upon a living soul,
The falcon preyeth not on a dead mouse.[13]

Love setteth a world aflame at every turn, and he wasteth every land where he carrieth his banner. Being hath no existence in his kingdom; the wise wield no command within his realm. The leviathan of love swalloweth the master of reason and destroyeth the lord of knowledge. He drinketh the seven seas, but his heart's thirst is still unquenched, and he saith, "Is there yet any more?"[14] He shunneth himself and draweth away from all on earth.

Love's a stranger to earth and heaven too;
In him are lunacies seventy-and-two.[15]

He hath bound a myriad victims in his fetters, wounded a myriad wise men with his arrow. Know that every redness in the world is from his anger, and every paleness in men's cheeks is

14. Qur'án 50:29
15. Jalálu'd-Dín Rúmí (1207-1273 A.D.); The *Mathnaví*. Jalálu'd-Dín, called Mawláná ("our Master"), is the greatest of all Persian Ṣúfí poets, and founder of the Mawlaví "whirling" dervish order.

from his poison. He yieldeth no remedy but death, he walketh not save in the valley of the shadow; yet sweeter than honey is his venom on the lover's lips, and fairer his destruction in the seeker's eyes than a hundred thousand lives.

Wherefore must the veils of the satanic self be burned away at the fire of love, that the spirit may be purified and cleansed and thus may know the station of the Lord of the Worlds.

> Kindle the fire of love and burn away all things,
> Then set thy foot into the land of the lovers.[16]

And if, confirmed by the Creator, the lover escapes from the claws of the eagle of love, he will enter

THE VALLEY OF KNOWLEDGE

and come out of doubt into certitude, and turn from the darkness of illusion to the guiding light of the fear of God. His inner eyes will open and he will privily converse with his Beloved; he will set ajar the gate of truth and piety, and shut the doors of vain imaginings.

16. From an ode by Bahá'u'lláh.

He in this station is content with the decree of
God, and seeth war as peace, and findeth in
death the secrets of everlasting life. With inward and outward eyes he witnesseth the mysteries of resurrection in the realms of creation
and the souls of men, and with a pure heart
apprehendeth the divine wisdom in the endless
Manifestations of God. In the ocean he findeth
a drop, in a drop he beholdeth the secrets of
the sea.

Split the atom's heart, and lo!
Within it thou wilt find a sun.[13]

The wayfarer in this Valley seeth in the
fashionings of the True One nothing save clear
providence, and at every moment saith: "No
defect canst thou see in the creation of the God
of Mercy: Repeat the gaze: Seest thou a single
flaw?"[17] He beholdeth justice in injustice, and
in justice, grace. In ignorance he findeth many
a knowledge hidden, and in knowledge a myriad
wisdoms manifest. He breaketh the cage of
the body and the passions, and consorteth with
the people of the immortal realm. He mounteth
on the ladders of inner truth and hasteneth to
the heaven of inner significance. He rideth in
the ark of "we shall show them our signs in

17. Qur'án 67:3.

the regions and in themselves,"[18] and journeyeth over the sea of "until it become plain to
them that (this Book) is the truth."[18] And if
he meeteth with injustice he shall have patience,
and if he cometh upon wrath he shall manifest
love.

There was once a lover who had sighed for
long years in separation from his beloved, and
wasted in the fire of remoteness. From the rule
of love, his heart was empty of patience, and
his body weary of his spirit; he reckoned life
without her as a mockery, and time consumed
him away. How many a day he found no rest
in longing for her; how many a night the pain
of her kept him from sleep; his body was worn
to a sigh, his heart's wound had turned him to
a cry of sorrow. He had given a thousand
lives for one taste of the cup of her presence,
but it availed him not. The doctors knew no
cure for him, and companions avoided his company; yea, physicians have no medicine for one
sick of love, unless the favor of the beloved
one deliver him.

At last, the tree of his longing yielded the
fruit of despair, and the fire of his hope fell
to ashes. Then one night he could live no more,
and he went out of his house and made for the
marketplace. On a sudden, a watchman fol-

18. Qur'án 41:53.

13

lowed after him. He broke into a run, with the watchman following; then other watchmen came together, and barred every passage to the weary one. And the wretched one cried from his heart, and ran here and there, and moaned to himself: "Surely this watchman is 'Izrá'íl, my angel of death, following so fast upon me; or he is a tyrant of men, seeking to harm me." His feet carried him on, the one bleeding with the arrow of love, and his heart lamented. Then he came to a garden wall, and with untold pain he scaled it, for it proved very high; and forgetting his life, he threw himself down to the garden.

And there he beheld his beloved with a lamp in her hand, searching for a ring she had lost. When the heart-surrendered lover looked on his ravishing love, he drew a great breath and raised up his hands in prayer, crying: "O God! Give Thou glory to the watchman, and riches and long life. For the watchman was Gabriel, guiding this poor one; or he was Isráfíl, bringing life to this wretched one!"

Indeed, his words were true, for he had found many a secret justice in this seeming tyranny of the watchman, and seen how many a mercy lay hid behind the veil. Out of wrath, the guard had led him who was athirst in love's desert to the sea of his loved one, and lit up the dark night of absence with the light of reunion. He had driven one who was afar, into the garden of nearness, had guided an ailing soul to the heart's physician.

Now if the lover could have looked ahead, he would have blessed the watchman at the start, and prayed on his behalf, and he would have seen that tyranny as justice; but since the end was veiled to him, he moaned and made his plaint in the beginning. Yet those who journey in the garden land of knowledge, because they see the end in the beginning, see peace in war and friendliness in anger.

Such is the state of the wayfarers in this Valley; but the people of the Valleys above this see the end and the beginning as one; nay, they see neither beginning nor end, and witness neither "first" nor "last."[19] Nay rather, the denizens of the undying city, who dwell in the green garden land, see not even "neither first nor last"; they fly from all that is first, and repulse all that is last. For these have passed over the worlds of names, and fled beyond the worlds of attributes as swift as lightning. Thus is it said: "Absolute Unity excludeth all attributes."[20] And they have made their dwelling-place in the shadow of the Essence.

19. Qur'án 57:3.
20. Saying attributed to 'Alí.

15

Wherefore, relevant to this, <u>Kh</u>ájih 'Abdu'-lláh[21]—may God the Most High sanctify his beloved spirit—hath made a subtle point and spoken an eloquent word as to the meaning of "Guide Thou us on the straight path,"[22] which is: "Show us the right way, that is, honor us with the love of Thine Essence, that we may be freed from turning toward ourselves and toward all else save Thee, and may become wholly Thine, and know only Thee, and see only Thee, and think of none save Thee."

Nay, these even mount above this station, wherefore it is said:

> Love is a veil betwixt the lover and the loved one;
> More than this I am not permitted to tell.[15]

At this hour the morn of knowledge hath arisen and the lamps of wayfaring and wandering are quenched.[23]

---

21. <u>Sh</u>ay<u>kh</u> Abú Ismá'íl 'Abdu'lláh Anṣárí of Hirát (1006-1088 A.D.) Ṣúfí leader, descended from the Prophet's companion Abú Ayyúb. Chiefly known for his *Munáját* (Supplications) and *Rubá'íyyát* (Quatrains). "Anṣár" means the "Helpers" or companions of Muḥammad in Medina.

22. Qur'án 1:5.

23. This refers to the mystic wandering and search for truth guided by "Lights" or Ṣúfí leaders. Bahá'u'lláh here warns the mystics that the coming of the Divine

Veiled from this was Moses
Though all strength and light;
Then thou who hast no wings at all,
Attempt not flight. [15]

If thou be a man of communion and prayer,
soar up on the wings of assistance from Holy
Souls, that thou mayest behold the mysteries
of the Friend and attain to the lights of the
Beloved. "Verily, we are from God and to Him
shall we return."[24]

After passing through the Valley of knowledge, which is the last plane of limitation, the
wayfarer cometh to

THE VALLEY OF UNITY

and drinketh from the cup of the Absolute,
and gazeth on the Manifestations of Oneness.
In this station he pierceth the veils of plurality,
fleeth from the worlds of the flesh, and ascend-
eth into the heaven of singleness. With the ear
of God he heareth, with the eye of God he
beholdeth the mysteries of divine creation. He
steppeth into the sanctuary of the Friend, and

Manifestation in His Day makes further search unneces-
sary, as it was said by 'Alí: "Quench the lamp when the sun
hath risen"—the sun referring to the Manifestation of God
in the New Day.

24. Qur'án 2:151.

shareth as an intimate the pavilion of the Loved One. He stretcheth out the hand of truth from the sleeve of the Absolute; he revealeth the secrets of power. He seeth in himself neither name nor fame nor rank, but findeth his own praise in praising God. He beholdeth in his own name the name of God; to him, "all songs are from the King,"[15] and every melody from Him. He sitteth on the throne of "Say, all is from God,"[25] and taketh his rest on the carpet of "There is no power or might but in God."[26] He looketh on all things with the eye of oneness, and seeth the brilliant rays of the divine sun shining from the dawning-point of Essence alike on all created things, and the lights of singleness reflected over all creation.

It is clear to thine Eminence that all the variations which the wayfarer in the stages of his journey beholdeth in the realms of being, proceed from his own vision. We shall give an example of this, that its meaning may become fully clear: Consider the visible sun; although it shineth with one radiance upon all things, and at the behest of the King of Manifestation bestoweth light on all creation, yet in each place it becometh manifest and sheddeth its

25. Qur'án 4:80.   26. Qur'án 18:37.

bounty according to the potentialities of that place. For instance, in a mirror it reflecteth its own disk and shape, and this is due to the sensitivity of the mirror; in a crystal it maketh fire to appear, and in other things it showeth only the effect of its shining, but not its full disk. And yet, through that effect, by the command of the Creator, it traineth each thing according to the quality of that thing, as thou observest.

In like manner, colors become visible in every object according to the nature of that object. For instance, in a yellow globe, the rays shine yellow; in a white the rays are white; and in a red, the red rays are manifest. Then these variations are from the object, not from the shining light. And if a place be shut away from the light, as by walls or a roof, it will be entirely bereft of the splendor of the light, nor will the sun shine thereon.

Thus it is that certain invalid souls have confined the lands of knowledge within the wall of self and passion, and clouded them with ignorance and blindness, and have been veiled from the light of the mystic sun and the mysteries of the Eternal Beloved; they have strayed afar from the jewelled wisdom of the lucid Faith of the Lord of Messengers, have been shut out of the sanctuary of the

19

All-Beauteous One, and banished from the Ka'bih[7] of splendor. Such is the worth of the people of this age!

And if a nightingale[27] soar upward from the clay of self and dwell in the rose bower of the heart, and in Arabian melodies and sweet Íránian songs recount the mysteries of God— a single word of which quickeneth to fresh, new life the bodies of the dead, and bestoweth the Holy Spirit upon the moldering bones of this existence—thou wilt behold a thousand claws of envy, a myriad beaks of rancor hunting after Him and with all their power intent upon His death.

Yea, to the beetle a sweet fragrance seemeth foul, and to the man sick of a rheum a pleasant perfume is as naught. Wherefore, it hath been said for the guidance of the ignorant:

Cleanse thou the rheum from out thine head
And breathe the breath of God instead.[15]

In sum, the differences in objects have now been made plain. Thus when the wayfarer gazeth only upon the place of appearance—that is, when he seeth only the many-colored globes —he beholdeth yellow and red and white; hence it is that conflict hath prevailed among the

27. This refers to Bahá'u'lláh's own Manifestation.

20

creatures, and a darksome dust from limited souls hath hid the world. And some do gaze upon the effulgence of the light; and some have drunk of the wine of oneness and these see nothing but the sun itself.

Thus, for that they move on these three differing planes, the understanding and the words of the wayfarers have differed; and hence the sign of conflict doth continually appear on earth. For some there are who dwell upon the plane of oneness and speak of that world, and some inhabit the realms of limitation, and some the grades of self, while others are completely veiled. Thus do the ignorant people of the day, who have no portion of the radiance of Divine Beauty, make certain claims, and in every age and cycle inflict on the people of the sea of oneness what they themselves deserve. "Should God punish men for their perverse doings, He would not leave on earth a moving thing! But to an appointed term doth He respite them. . . ."[28]

O My Brother! A pure heart is as a mirror; cleanse it with the burnish of love and severance from all save God, that the true sun may shine within it and the eternal morning dawn. Then wilt thou clearly see the meaning of "Neither doth My earth nor My heaven contain Me,

28. Qur'án 16:63.

21

but the heart of My faithful servant containeth Me."[29] And thou wilt take up thy life in thine hand, and with infinite longing cast it before the new Beloved One.

Whensoever the light of Manifestation of the King of Oneness settleth upon the throne of the heart and soul, His shining becometh visible in every limb and member. At that time the mystery of the famed tradition gleameth out of the darkness: "A servant is drawn unto Me in prayer until I answer him; and when I have answered him, I become the ear wherewith he heareth. . . ." For thus the Master of the house hath appeared within His home, and all the pillars of the dwelling are ashine with His light. And the action and effect of the light are from the Light-Giver; so it is that all move through Him and arise by His will. And this is that spring whereof the near ones drink, as it is said: "A fount whereof the near unto God shall drink. . . ."[30]

However, let none construe these utterances to be anthropomorphism, nor see in them the descent of the worlds of God into the grades of the creatures; nor should they lead thine Eminence to such assumptions. For God is, in

29. Ḥadíth, i.e. action or utterance traditionally attributed to the the Prophet Muhammad or to one of the holy Imáms.

30. Qur'án 83:28.

22

His Essence, holy above ascent and descent, entrance and exit; He hath through all eternity been free of the attributes of human creatures, and ever will remain so. No man hath ever known Him; no soul hath ever found the pathway to His Being. Every mystic knower hath wandered far astray in the valley of the knowledge of Him; every saint hath lost his way in seeking to comprehend His Essence. Sanctified is He above the understanding of the wise; exalted is He above the knowledge of the knowing! The way is barred and to seek it is impiety; His proof is His signs; His being is His evidence.[4]

Wherefore, the lovers of the face of the Beloved have said: "O Thou, the One Whose Essence alone showeth the way to His Essence, and Who is sanctified above any likeness to His creatures."[29] How can utter nothingness gallop its steed in the field of preexistence, or a fleeting shadow reach to the everlasting sun? The Friend[31] hath said, "But for Thee, we had not known Thee," and the Beloved[31] hath said, "nor attained Thy presence."

Yea, these mentionings that have been made of the grades of knowledge relate to the knowledge of the Manifestations of that Sun of Reality, which casteth Its light upon the Mir-

31. The Prophet Muḥammad.

23

rors. And the splendor of that light is in the hearts, yet it is hidden under the veilings of sense and the conditions of this earth, even as a candle within a lantern of iron, and only when the lantern is removed doth the light of the candle shine out.

In like manner, when thou strippest the wrappings of illusion from off thine heart, the lights of oneness will be made manifest.

Then it is clear that even for the rays there is neither entrance nor exit—how much less for that Essence of Being and that longed-for Mystery. O My Brother, journey upon these planes in the spirit of search, not in blind imitation. A true wayfarer will not be kept back by the bludgeon of words nor debarred by the warning of allusions.

How shall a curtain part the lover and the
  loved one?
Not Alexander's wall can separate them![32]

Secrets are many, but strangers are myriad. Volumes will not suffice to hold the mystery of the Beloved One, nor can it be exhausted in these pages, although it be no more than a word, no more than a sign. ''Knowledge is a

32. Ḥáfiẓ: Shamsu'd-Dín Muḥammad, of Shíráz, died ca. 1389 A.D. One of the greatest of Persian poets.

24

single point, but the ignorant have multiplied it."[29]

On this same basis, ponder likewise the differences among the worlds. Although the divine worlds be never ending, yet some refer to them as four: The world of time (*zamán*), which is the one that hath both a beginning and an end; the world of duration (*dahr*), which hath a beginning, but whose end is not revealed; the world of perpetuity (*darmad*), whose beginning is not to be seen but which is known to have an end; and the world of eternity (*azal*), neither a beginning nor an end of which is visible. Although there are many differing statements as to these points, to recount them in detail would result in weariness. Thus, some have said that the world of perpetuity hath neither beginning nor end, and have named the world of eternity as the invisible, impregnable Empyrean. Others have called these the worlds of the Heavenly Court (Láhút), of the Empyrean Heaven (Jabarút), of the Kingdom of the Angels (Malakút), and of the mortal world (Násút).

The journeys in the pathway of love are reckoned as four: From the creatures to the True One; from the True One to the creatures; from the creatures to the creatures; from the True One to the True One.

There is many an utterance of the mystic seers and doctors of former times which I have not mentioned here, since I mislike the copious citation from sayings of the past; for quotation from the words of others proveth acquired learning, not the divine bestowal. Even so much as We have quoted here is out of deference to the wont of men and after the manner of the friends. Further, such matters are beyond the scope of this epistle. Our unwillingness to recount their sayings is not from pride, rather is it a manifestation of wisdom and a demonstration of grace.

> If Khiḍr did wreck the vessel on the sea,
> Yet in this wrong there are a thousand rights.[15]

Otherwise, this Servant regardeth Himself as utterly lost and as nothing, even beside one of the beloved of God, how much less in the presence of His holy ones. Exalted be My Lord, the Supreme! Moreover, our aim is to recount the stages of the wayfarer's journey, not to set forth the conflicting utterances of the mystics.

Although a brief example hath been given concerning the beginning and ending of the relative world, the world of attributes, yet a second illustration is now added, that the full meaning may be manifest. For instance, let thine Eminence consider his own self; thou art first in relation to thy son, last in relation to thy father. In thine outward appearance, thou tellest of the appearance of power in the realms of divine creation; in thine inward being thou revealest the hidden mysteries which are the divine trust deposited within thee. And thus firstness and lastness, outwardness and inwardness are, in the sense referred to, true of thyself, that in these four states conferred upon thee thou shouldst comprehend the four divine states, and that the nightingale of thine heart on all the branches of the rosetree of existence, whether visible or concealed, should cry out: "He is the first and the last, the Seen and the Hidden. . . ."[33]

These statements are made in the sphere of that which is relative, because of the limitations of men. Otherwise, those personages who in a single step have passed over the world of the relative and the limited, and dwelt on the fair plane of the Absolute, and pitched their tent in the worlds of authority and command—have burned away these relativities with a single spark, and blotted out these words with a drop

33. Qur'án 57:3.

27

of dew. And they swim in the sea of the spirit, and soar in the holy air of light. Then what life have words, on such a plane, that "first" and "last" or other than these be seen or mentioned! In this realm, the first is the last itself, and the last is but the first.

In thy soul of love build thou a fire
And burn all thoughts and words entire.[15]

O my friend, look upon thyself: Hadst thou not become a father nor begotten a son, neither wouldst thou have heard these sayings. Now forget them all, that thou mayest learn from the Master of Love in the schoolhouse of oneness, and return unto God, and forsake the inner land of unreality[34] for thy true station, and dwell within the shadow of the tree of knowledge.

O thou dear one! Impoverish thyself, that thou mayest enter the high court of riches; and humble thy body, that thou mayest drink from the river of glory, and attain to the full meaning of the poems whereof thou hadst asked.

Thus it hath been made clear that these stages depend on the vision of the wayfarer. In every city he will behold a world, in every Valley

34. This refers to the Ṣúfí idea of the inner plane, which compared to Revealed Truth is but unreal.

reach a spring, in every meadow hear a song. But the falcon of the mystic heaven hath many a wondrous carol of the spirit in His breast, and the Persian bird keepeth in His soul many a sweet Arab melody; yet these are hidden, and hidden shall remain.

If I speak forth, many a mind will shatter,
And if I write, many a pen will break.[15,35]

Peace be upon him who concludeth this exalted journey and followeth the True One by the lights of guidance.

And the wayfarer, after traversing the high planes of this supernal journey, entereth

THE VALLEY OF CONTENTMENT

In this Valley he feeleth the winds of divine contentment blowing from the plane of the spirit. He burneth away the veils of want, and with inward and outward eye, perceiveth within and without all things the day of: ''God will compensate each one out of His abundance.''[36] From sorrow he turneth to bliss, from anguish to joy. His grief and mourning yield to delight and rapture.

35. This refers to Bahá'u'lláh Himself, Who had not yet declared His mission.
36. Qur'án 4:129.

Although to outward view, the wayfarers in this Valley may dwell upon the dust, yet inwardly they are throned in the heights of mystic meaning; they eat of the endless bounties of inner significances, and drink of the delicate wines of the spirit.

The tongue faileth in describing these three Valleys, and speech falleth short. The pen steppeth not into this region, the ink leaveth only a blot. In these planes, the nightingale of the heart hath other songs and secrets, which make the heart to stir and the soul to clamor, but this mystery of inner meaning may be whispered only from heart to heart, confided only from breast to breast.

> Only heart to heart can speak the bliss of
>   mystic knowers;
> No messenger can tell it and no missive bear
>   it.[32]

> I am silent from weakness on many a matter,
> For my words could not reckon them and my
>   speech would fall short.[37]

O friend, till thou enter the garden of such mysteries, thou shalt never set lip to the undying wine of this Valley. And shouldst thou

37. Arabian poem.

taste of it, thou wilt shield thine eyes from all things else, and drink of the wine of contentment; and thou wilt loose thyself from all things else, and bind thyself to Him, and throw thy life down in His path, and cast thy soul away. However, there is no other in this region that thou need forget: "There was God and there was naught beside Him."[29] For on this plane the traveler witnesseth the beauty of the Friend in everything. Even in fire, he seeth the face of the Beloved. He beholdeth in illusion the secret of reality, and readeth from the attributes the riddle of the Essence. For he hath burnt away the veils with his sighing, and unwrapped the shroudings with a single glance; with piercing sight he gazeth on the new creation; with lucid heart he graspeth subtle verities. This is sufficiently attested by: "And we have made thy sight sharp in this day."[38]

After journeying through the planes of pure contentment, the traveler cometh to

THE VALLEY OF WONDERMENT

and is tossed in the oceans of grandeur, and at every moment his wonder groweth. Now he seeth the shape of wealth as poverty itself, and the essence of freedom as sheer impotence.

38. From Qur'án 50:21.

Now is he struck dumb with the beauty of the All-Glorious; again is he wearied out with his own life. How many a mystic tree hath this whirlwind of wonderment snatched by the roots, how many a soul hath it exhausted. For in this Valley the traveler is flung into confusion, albeit, in the eye of him who hath attained, such marvels are esteemed and well beloved. At every moment he beholdeth a wondrous world, a new creation, and goeth from astonishment to astonishment, and is lost in awe at the works of the Lord of Oneness.

Indeed, O Brother, if we ponder each created thing, we shall witness a myriad perfect wisdoms and learn a myriad new and wondrous truths. One of the created phenomena is the dream. Behold how many secrets are deposited therein, how many wisdoms treasured up, how many worlds concealed. Observe, how thou art asleep in a dwelling, and its doors are barred; on a sudden thou findest thyself in a far-off city, which thou enterest without moving thy feet or wearying thy body; without using thine eyes, thou seest; without taxing thine ears, thou hearest; without a tongue, thou speakest. And perchance when ten years are gone, thou wilt witness in the outer world the very things thou hast dreamed tonight.

Now there are many wisdoms to ponder in

the dream, which none but the people of this Valley can comprehend in their true elements. First, what is this world, where without eye and ear and hand and tongue, a man puts all of these to use? Second, how is it that in the outer world thou seest today the effect of a dream, when thou didst vision it in the world of sleep some ten years past? Consider the difference between these two worlds and the mysteries which they conceal, that thou mayest attain to divine confirmations and heavenly discoveries and enter the regions of holiness.

God, the Exalted, hath placed these signs in men, to the end that philosophers may not deny the mysteries of the life beyond nor belittle that which hath been promised them. For some hold to reason and deny whatever the reason comprehendeth not, and yet weak minds can never grasp the matters which we have related, but only the Supreme, Divine Intelligence can comprehend them:

How can feeble reason encompass the
Qur'án,
Or the spider snare a phoenix in his web?[13]

All these states are to be witnessed in the Valley of Wonderment, and the traveler at every moment seeketh for more, and is not wearied. Thus the Lord of the First and the Last in setting forth the grades of contemplation, and expressing wonderment hath said: "O Lord, increase my astonishment at Thee!"

Likewise, reflect upon the perfection of man's creation, and that all these planes and states are folded up and hidden away within him.

> Dost thou reckon thyself only a puny form
> When within thee the universe is folded?[39]

Then we must labor to destroy the animal condition, till the meaning of humanity shall come to light.

Thus, too, Luqmán, who had drunk from the wellspring of wisdom and tasted of the waters of mercy, in proving to his son Nathan the planes of resurrection and death, advanced the dream as an evidence and an example. We relate it here, that through this evanescent Servant a memory may endure of that youth of the school of Divine Unity, that elder of the art of instruction and the Absolute. He said: "O Son, if thou art able not to sleep, then thou art able not to die. And if thou art able not

39. 'Alí.

34

to waken after sleep, then thou shalt be able not to rise after death.''

O friend, the heart is the dwelling of eternal mysteries, make it not the home of fleeting fancies; waste not the treasure of thy precious life in employment with this swiftly passing world. Thou comest from the world of holiness—bind not thine heart to the earth; thou art a dweller in the court of nearness—choose not the homeland of the dust.

In sum, there is no end to the description of these stages, but because of the wrongs inflicted by the peoples of the earth, this Servant is in no mood to continue:

> The tale is still unfinished and I have no
>   heart for it—
> Then pray forgive me.[15]

The pen groaneth and the ink sheddeth tears, and the river[40] of the heart moveth in waves of blood. ''Nothing can befall us but what God hath destined for us.''[41] Peace be upon him who followeth the Right Path!

After scaling the high summits of wonderment the wayfarer cometh to

40. Literally ''Jayḥún,'' a river in Turkistán.
41. Qur'án 9:51.

THE VALLEY OF TRUE POVERTY
AND ABSOLUTE NOTHINGNESS

This station is the dying from self and the living in God, the being poor in self and rich in the Desired One. Poverty as here referred to signifieth being poor in the things of the created world, rich in the things of God's world. For when the true lover and devoted friend reacheth to the presence of the Beloved, the sparkling beauty of the Loved One and the fire of the lover's heart will kindle a blaze and burn away all veils and wrappings. Yea, all he hath, from heart to skin, will be set aflame, so that nothing will remain save the Friend.

> When the qualities of the Ancient of Days stood revealed,
> Then the qualities of earthly things did Moses burn away.[15]

He who hath attained this station is sanctified from all that pertaineth to the world. Wherefore, if those who have come to the sea of His presence are found to possess none of the limited things of this perishable world, whether it be outer wealth or personal opinions, it mattereth not. For whatever the creatures have is limited by their own limits, and whatever the

True One hath is sanctified therefrom; this utterance must be deeply pondered that its purport may be clear. "Verily the righteous shall drink of a winecup tempered at the camphor fountain."[42] If the interpretation of "camphor" become known, the true intention will be evident. This state is that poverty of which it is said, "Poverty is My glory."[43] And of inward and outward poverty there is many a stage and many a meaning which I have not thought pertinent to mention here; hence I have reserved these for another time, dependent on what God may desire and fate may seal.

This is the plane whereon the vestiges of all things (Kullu Shay') are destroyed in the traveler, and on the horizon of eternity the Divine Face riseth out of the darkness, and the meaning of "All on the earth shall pass away, but the face of thy Lord. . . ."[44] is made manifest.

O My friend, listen with heart and soul to the songs of the spirit, and treasure them as thine own eyes. For the heavenly wisdoms, like the clouds of spring, will not rain down on the earth of men's hearts forever; and though the grace of the All-Bounteous One is never stilled and never ceasing, yet to each time and era a

42. Qur'án 76:5.   44. Qur'án 55:26, 27.
43. Muhammad.

portion is allotted and a bounty set apart, this in a given measure. "And no one thing is there, but with Us are its storehouses; and We send it not down but in settled measure."[45] The cloud of the Loved One's mercy raineth only on the garden of the spirit, and bestoweth this bounty only in the season of spring. The other seasons have no share in this greatest grace, and barren lands no portion of this favor.

O Brother! Not every sea hath pearls; not every branch will flower, nor will the nightingale sing thereon. Then, ere the nightingale of the mystic paradise repair to the garden of God, and the rays of the heavenly morning return to the Sun of Truth—make thou an effort, that haply in this dustheap of the mortal world thou mayest catch a fragrance from the everlasting garden, and live forever in the shadow of the peoples of this city. And when thou hast attained this highest station and come to this mightiest plane, then shalt thou gaze on the Beloved, and forget all else.

The Beloved shineth on gate and wall
Without a veil, O men of vision.[12]

Now hast thou abandoned the drop of life and come to the sea of the Life-Bestower.

45. Qur'án 15:21.

This is the goal thou didst ask for; if it be God's will, thou wilt gain it.

In this city, even the veils of light are split asunder and vanish away. "His beauty hath no veiling save light, His face no covering save revelation."[29] How strange that while the Beloved is visible as the sun, yet the heedless still hunt after tinsel and base metal. Yea, the intensity of His revelation hath covered Him, and the fullness of His shining forth hath hidden Him.

> Even as the sun, bright hath He shined,
> But alas, He hath come to the town of the
>   blind![15]

In this Valley, the wayfarer leaveth behind him the stages of the "oneness of Being and Manifestation"[46] and reacheth a oneness that is sanctified above these two stations. Ecstasy alone can encompass this theme, not utterance nor argument; and whosoever hath dwelt at this stage of the journey, or caught a breath from this garden land, knoweth whereof We speak.

In all these journeys the traveler must stray

46. Pantheism, a Ṣúfí doctrine derived from the formula: "Only God exists; He is in all things, and all things are in Him."

not the breadth of a hair from the "Law," for this is indeed the secret of the "Path" and the fruit of the Tree of "Truth"; and in all these stages he must cling to the robe of obedience to the commandments, and hold fast to the cord of shunning all forbidden things, that he may be nourished from the cup of the Law and informed of the mysteries of Truth.[47]

If any of the utterances of this Servant may not be comprehended, or may lead to perturbation, the same must be inquired of again, that no doubt may linger, and the meaning be clear as the Face of the Beloved One shining from the "Glorious Station."[48]

These journeys have no visible ending in the world of time, but the severed wayfarer—if invisible confirmation descend upon him and the Guardian of the Cause assist him—may cross these seven stages in seven steps, nay rather in seven breaths, nay rather in a single

---

47. This refers to the three stages of Ṣúfí life: 1. Sharí'at, or Religious Laws; 2. Ṭaríqat, or the Path on which the mystic wayfarer journeys in search of the True One; this stage also includes anchoretism. 3. Ḥaqíqat, or the Truth which, to the Ṣúfí, is the goal of the journey through all three stages. Here Bahá'u'lláh teaches that, contrary to the belief of certain Ṣúfís who in their search for the Truth consider themselves above all law, obedience to the Laws of Religion is essential.

48. *Maqám-i-Maḥmúd.* Qur'án 17:81.

breath, if God will and desire it. And this is of "His grace on such of His servants as He pleaseth."[49]

They who soar in the heaven of singleness and reach to the sea of the Absolute, reckon this city—which is the station of life in God—as the furthermost state of mystic knowers, and the farthest homeland of the lovers. But to this evanescent One of the mystic ocean, this station is the first gate of the heart's citadel, that is, man's first entrance to the city of the heart; and the heart is endowed with four stages, which would be recounted should a kindred soul be found.

When the pen set to picturing this station,
It broke in pieces and the page was torn.[13]

Salám![50]

O My friend! Many a hound pursueth this gazelle of the desert of oneness; many a talon claweth at this thrush of the eternal garden. Pitiless ravens do lie in wait for this bird of the heavens of God, and the huntsman of envy stalketh this deer of the meadow of love.

O Shaykh! Make of thine effort a glass, perchance it may shelter this flame from the

49. Qur'án 2:84.
50. "Peace." This word is used in concluding a thesis.

contrary winds; albeit this light doth long to be kindled in the lamp of the Lord, and to shine in the globe of the spirit. For the head raised up in the love of God will certainly fall by the sword, and the life that is kindled with longing will surely be sacrificed, and the heart which remembereth the Loved One will surely brim with blood. How well is it said:

> Live free of love, for its very peace is
>   anguish;
> Its beginning is pain, its end is death.[37]

Peace be upon him who followeth the Right Path!

*   *   *   *   *   *

The thoughts thou hast expressed as to the interpretation of the common species of bird that is called in Persian Gunjishk (sparrow) were considered.[51] Thou appearest to be well-grounded in mystic truth. However, on every plane, to every letter a meaning is allotted which relateth to that plane. Indeed, the wayfarer findeth a secret in every name, a mystery in every letter. In one sense, these letters refer to holiness.

Káf or *Gáf* (K or G) referreth to *Kuffi*

---

51. The five letters comprising this word in Persian are: G, N, J, SH, K, that is, *Gáf, Nún, Jím, Shín, Káf.*

("free"), that is, "Free thyself from that which thy passion desireth; then advance unto thy Lord."

Nún referreth to *Nazzih* ("purify"), that is, "Purify thyself from all else save Him, that thou mayest surrender thy life in His love."

Jím is *Jánib* ("draw back"), that is, "Draw back from the threshold of the True One if thou still possessest earthly attributes."

Shín is *Ushkur* ("thank")—"Thank thy Lord on His earth that He may bless thee in His heaven; albeit in the world of oneness, this heaven is the same as His earth."

Káf referreth to *Kuffi*, that is: "Take off from thyself the wrappings of limitations, that thou mayest come to know what thou hast not known of the states of Sanctity."[52]

Wert thou to harken to the melodies of this mortal Bird,[53] then wouldst thou seek out the undying chalice and pass by every perishable cup.

Peace be upon those who walk in the Right Path!

52. This and the foregoing quotations are from the teachings of Islám.

53. This is a reference in the traditional Persian style to Bahá'u'lláh Himself.

43

THE FOUR VALLEYS

THE FOUR VALLEYS

He is the Strong, the Well-Beloved!

O light of truth, Ḥisám-i-Dín, the bounteous,
No prince hath the world begot like unto
Thee![1]

I am wondering why the tie of love was so
abruptly severed, and the firm covenant of
friendship broken. Did ever, God forbid, My
devotion lessen, or My deep affection fail, that
thou hast thus forgot Me and blotted Me from
thy thoughts?

What fault of Mine hath made thee cease thy
favors?
Is it that We are lowly and thou of high
degree?[2]

1. *Mathnaví* of Rúmí.
2. Sa'dí, Muṣliḥu'd-Dín of Shíráz (ca. 1184-1291),
famed author of the *Gulistán* and other poetical works.

47

Or is that a single arrow hath driven thee from the battle?[3] Have they not told thee that faithfulness is a duty on those who follow the mystic way, that it is the true guide to His Holy Presence? "But as for those who say, 'Our Lord is God,' and who go straight to Him, the angels shall descend to them. . . ."[4]

Likewise He saith, "Go straight on then as thou hast been commanded."[5] Wherefore, this course is incumbent on those who dwell in the presence of God.

> I do as bidden, and I bring the message,
> Whether it give thee counsel or offense.[6]

Albeit I have received no answer to My letters and it is contrary to the usage of the wise to express My regard anew, yet this new love hath broken all the old rules and ways.

> Tell us not the tale of Laylí or of Majnún's woe—
> Thy love hath made the world forget the loves of long ago.

3. Persian proverb describing a man who gives up easily. As used here one connotation is that the Shaykh might have considered his station as a mystic leader compromised by the fact of his being taught the new truth by Bahá'u'lláh.

4. Qur'án 41:30.

5. Qur'án 11:114; 42:14.

6. Sa'dí.

When once thy name was on the tongue, the
  lovers caught it
And it set the speakers and the hearers danc-
  ing to and fro.[7]

And of divine wisdom and heavenly counsel,
[Rúmí says]:

Each moon, O my beloved, for three days I
  go mad;
Today's the first of these—'Tis why thou
  seest me glad.

We hear that thou hast journeyed to Tabríz and Tiflis to disseminate knowledge, or
that some other high purpose hath taken thee to
Sanandaj.[8,9]

O My eminent friend! Those who progress
in mystic wayfaring are of four kinds. I shall
describe them in brief, that the grades and
qualities of each kind may become plain to
thee.

7. Ibid.
8. Senna, capital of Persian Kurdistán.
9. This preamble to the *Four Valleys* is written in the
finest Persian epistolary style. The rules of classical letter
writing in Persian require quotations from literary works,
and assertions of abiding love for the one addressed, who is
chided for having neglected the writer.

THE FIRST VALLEY

If the travelers seek after the goal of the Intended One (*maqṣúd*), this station appertaineth to the self—but that self which is "The Self of God standing within Him with laws."[10]

On this plane, the self is not rejected but beloved; it is well-pleasing and not to be shunned. Although at the beginning, this plane is the realm of conflict, yet it endeth in attainment to the throne of splendor. As they have said: "O Abraham of this day, O Friend Abraham of the Spirit! Kill these four birds of prey,"[11] that after death the riddle of life may be unraveled.

This is the plane of the self that is well-pleasing unto God. Refer to the verse:

Oh, thou soul which art at rest,
Return to thy Lord, well-pleased, and pleasing Him:[12]

which endeth:

Enter thou among My servants,
And enter thou My paradise.[12]

10. Ḥadíth.

11. The *Mathnaví*. Here Rúmí tells a story of four evil birds which, when put to death, changed into four birds of goodness. The allegory refers to subduing evil qualities and replacing them with good.

12. Qur'án 89:27-30.

This station hath many signs, unnumbered proofs. Hence it is said: "Hereafter We will show them Our signs in the regions of the earth, and in themselves, until it become manifest unto them that it is the truth,"[13] and that there is no God save Him.

One must, then, read the book of his own self, rather than some treatise on rhetoric. Wherefore He hath said, "Read thy Book: There needeth none but thyself to make out an account against thee this day."[14]

The story is told of a mystic knower, who went on a journey with a learned grammarian as his companion. They came to the shore of the Sea of Grandeur. The knower straightway flung himself into the waves, but the grammarian stood lost in his reasonings, which were as words that are written on water. The knower called out to him, "Why dost thou not follow?" The grammarian answered, "O Brother, I dare not advance. I must needs go back again." Then the knower cried, "Forget what thou didst read in the books of Síbavayh and Qawlavayh, of Ibn-i-Hájib and Ibn-i-Málik,[15] and cross the water."

---

13. Qur'án 41:53.
14. Qur'án 17:15.
15. Famed writers on grammar and rhetoric.

The death of self is needed here, not rhetoric:
Be nothing, then, and walk upon the waves.[16]

Likewise is it written, "And be ye not like those who forget God, and whom He hath therefore caused to forget their own selves. These are the wicked doers."[17]

THE SECOND VALLEY

If the wayfarer's goal be the dwelling of the Praiseworthy One (Maḥmúd),[18] this is the station of primal reason which is known as the Prophet and the Most Great Pillar.[19] Here reason signifieth the divine, universal mind, whose sovereignty enlighteneth all created things—nor doth it refer to every feeble brain; for it is as the wise Saná'í hath written:

How can feeble reason encompass the Qur'án,
Or the spider snare a phoenix in his web?
Wouldst thou that the mind should not entrap thee?
Teach it the science of the love of God!

16. The *Mathnaví*.   17. Qur'án 59:19.
18. An attribute of God and one of the titles of Muḥammad.
19. *Maqám-i-Maḥmúd*–Praiseworthy Station—is the rank of Prophets endowed with constancy.

On this plane, the traveler meeteth with many a trial and reverse. Now is he lifted up to heaven, now is he cast into the depths. As it hath been said: "Now Thou drawest me to the summit of glory, again Thou casteth me into the lowest abyss." The mystery treasured in this plane is divulged in the following holy verse from the Súrih of THE CAVE:[20]

"And thou mightest have seen the sun when it arose, pass on the right of their cave, and when it set, leave them on the left, while they were in its spacious chamber. This is one of the signs of God. Guided indeed is he whom God guideth; but for him whom He misleadeth, thou shalt by no means find a patron."

If a man could know what lieth hid in this one verse, it would suffice him. Wherefore, in praise of such as these, He hath said: "Men whom neither merchandise nor traffic beguile from the remembrance of God. . . ."[21]

This station conferreth the true standard of knowledge, and freeth man from tests. In this realm, to search after knowledge is irrelevant, for He hath said concerning the guidance of travelers on this plane, "Fear God, and God

20. Qur'án 18:16. This is a reference to the station of complete faith. The companions of the Cave are identified with early Christian martyrs.
21. Qur'án 24:37.

will instruct thee.''[22] And again: ''Knowledge is a light which God casteth into the heart of whomsoever He willeth.''[23]

Wherefore, a man should make ready his heart that it be worthy of the descent of heavenly grace, and that the bounteous Cup-Bearer may give him to drink of the wine of bestowal from the merciful vessel. ''For the like of this let the travailers travail!''[24]

And now do I say, ''Verily we are from God, and to Him shall we return.''[25]

THE THIRD VALLEY

If the loving seekers wish to live within the precincts of the Attracting One (Majdhúb),[26] no soul may dwell on this Kingly Throne save the beauty of love. This realm is not to be pictured in words.

Love shunneth this world and that world too,
In him are lunacies seventy-and-two.
The minstrel of love harpeth this lay:
Servitude enslaveth, kingship doth betray.[27]

22. Qur'án 2:282.   24. Qur'án 37:59.
23. Hadíth.   25. Qur'án 2:151.
26. That attribute of God which draws all creatures to Him.
27. The Mathnaví.

This plane requireth pure affection and the bright stream of fellowship. In telling of these companions of the Cave He saith: "They speak not till He hath spoken; and they do His bidding."[28]

On this plane, neither the reign of reason is sufficient nor the authority of self. Hence, one of the Prophets of God hath asked: "O my Lord, how shall we reach unto Thee?" And the answer came, "Leave thyself behind, and then approach Me."

These are a people who deem the lowest place to be one with the throne of glory, and to them beauty's bower differeth not from the field of a battle fought in the cause of the Beloved.

The denizens of this plane speak no words—but they gallop their chargers. They see but the inner reality of the Beloved. To them all words of sense are meaningless, and senseless words are full of meaning. They cannot tell one limb from another, one part from another. To them the mirage is the real river; to them going away is returning. Wherefore hath it been said:

The story of Thy beauty reached the hermit's dell;

28. Qur'án 21:27.

Crazed, he sought the Tavern where the
wine they buy and sell.
The love of Thee hath leveled down the fort
of patience,
The pain of Thee hath firmly barred the gate
of hope as well.[29]

In this realm, instruction is assuredly of no
avail.

The lover's teacher is the Loved One's
beauty,
His face their lesson and their only book.
Learning of wonderment, of longing love
their duty,
Not on learned chapters and dull themes they
look.
The chain that binds them is His musky hair,
The Cyclic Scheme,[30] to them, is but to Him
a stair.[31]

Here followeth a supplication to God, the
Exalted, the Glorified:

29. Sa'dí.
30. The Cyclic Theory of Abu-'Alí Síná (Avicenna—
980–1037) as expressed by him in the quatrain:
  Every semblance, every shape that perisheth today
  In the treasure-house of Time is safely stored away.
  When the world revolveth to its former place,
  Out of the Invisible He draweth forth its face.
See also *Some Answered Questions*, p. 326.
  31. The *Mathnaví*.

O Lord! O Thou Whose bounty granteth
    wishes!
I stand before Thee, all save Thee forgetting.
Grant that the mote of knowledge in my
    spirit
Escape desire and the lowly clay;
Grant that Thine ancient gift, this drop of
    wisdom,
Merge with Thy mighty sea.[32]

Thus do I say: There is no power or might
save in God, the Protector, the Self-Subsis-
tent.[33]

THE FOURTH VALLEY

If the mystic knowers be of those who have
reached to the beauty of the Beloved One
(Maḥbúb), this station is the apex of con-
sciousness and the secret of divine guidance.
This is the center of the mystery: "He doth
what He willeth, ordaineth what He pleaseth."[34]

Were all the denizens of earth and heaven
to unravel this shining allusion, this darksome
riddle, until the Day when the Trumpet sound-

32. Ibid.
33. From Qur'án 18:37.
34. Qur'án 2:254; 5:1, etc.

eth, yet would they fail to comprehend even a letter thereof, for this is the station of God's immutable decree, His foreordained mystery. Hence, when searchers inquired of this, He made reply, "This is a bottomless sea which none shall ever fathom."[35] And they asked again, and He answered, "It is the blackest of nights through which none can find his way."

Whoso knoweth this secret will assuredly hide it, and were he to reveal but its faintest trace they would nail him to the cross. Yet, by the Living God, were there any true seeker, I would divulge it to him; for they have said: "Love is a light that never dwelleth in a heart possessed by fear."

Verily, the wayfarer who journeyeth unto God, unto the Crimson Pillar in the snow-white path, will never reach unto his heavenly goal unless he abandoneth all that men possess: "And if he feareth not God, God will make him to fear all things; whereas all things fear him who feareth God."[36]

> Speak in the Persian tongue, though the Arab please thee more;
> A lover hath many a tongue at his command.[37]

35. Statement attributed to 'Alí.
36. This quotation is in Arabic.
37. The *Mathnaví*.

How sweet is this couplet which revealeth such a truth:

See, our hearts come open like shells, when
   He raineth grace like pearls,
And our lives are ready targets, when
   agony's arrows He hurls.

And were it not contrary to the Law of the Book, I would verily bequeath a part of My possessions to the one who would put Me to death, and I would name him My heir; yea, I would bestow upon him a portion, would render him thanks, would seek to refresh Mine eyes with the touch of his hand. But what can I do? I have no possessions, no power, and this is what God hath ordained.[38]

Methinks at this moment, I catch the fragrance of His garment[39] blowing from the Egypt of Bahá;[40] verily He seemeth near at hand, though men may think Him far away.[41] My soul doth smell the perfume shed by the

38. This was revealed before the Declaration of Bahá'u'lláh. The lines following refer to the imminence of His Manifestation.

39. Literally, the garment of *Há*, which is the letter "H" and here represents Bahá.

40. This reference is to the story of Joseph in the Qur'án and the Bible.

41. This refers to those who did not expect the imminent advent of Him Whom God Shall Manifest.

Beloved One; My sense is filled with the fragrance of My dear Companion.

The duty of long years of love obey
And tell the tale of happy days gone by,
That land and sky may laugh aloud today,
And it may gladden mind and heart and
eye. [42]

This is the realm of full awareness, of utter self-effacement. Even love is no pathway to this region, and longing hath no dwelling here; wherefore is it said, "Love is a veil betwixt the lover and the beloved." Here love becometh an obstruction and a barrier, and all else save Him is but a curtain. The wise Saná'í hath written:

Never the covetous heart shall come to the
stealer of hearts,
Never the shrouded soul unite with beauty's
rose.

For this is the realm of Absolute Command and is free of all the attributes of earth.

The exalted dwellers in this mansion do wield divine authority in the court of rapture, with utter gladness, and they do bear a kingly

42. The *Mathnaví*.

sceptre. On the high seats of justice, they issue
their commands, and they send down gifts according to each man's deserving. Those who
drink of this cup abide in the high bowers of
splendor above the Throne of the Ancient of
Days, and they sit in the Empyrean of Might
within the Lofty Pavilion: "Naught shall they
know of sun or piercing cold."[43]

Herein the high heavens are in no conflict
with the lowly earth, nor do they seek to excel
it, for this is the land of mercy, not the realm
of distinction. Albeit at every moment these
souls appear in a new office, yet their condition
is ever the same. Wherefore of this realm it is
written, "No work withholdeth Him from another."[44] And of another state it is said:
"Every day doth some new work employ
Him."[45] This is the food whose savor chang-
eth not, whose color altereth not. If thou eatest
thereof, thou shalt verily chant this verse: "I
turn my face to Him Who hath created the
Heavens and the earth . . . I am not one of
those who add gods to God."[46] "And thus did
we show Abraham the Kingdom of the Heavens and of the Earth, that He might be estab-

43. Qur'án 76:13.
44. This quotation is from one of the commentators on
Qur'án 55:29. Cf. the dictionary *Lisánu'l-'Arab*.
45. Qur'án 55:29.
46. Qur'án 6:79.

lished in knowledge."[47] Wherefore, put thy hand into thy bosom, then stretch it forth with power, and behold, thou shalt find it a light unto all the world."[48]

How crystal this cool water that the Cup-Bearer bringeth! How bright this pure wine in the hands of the Beloved! How delicate this draught from the Heavenly Cup! May it do them good, whoso drink thereof, and taste of its sweetness and attain to its knowledge.

It is not fitting that I tell thee more,
For the stream's bed cannot hold the sea.[49]

For the mystery of this utterance is hid within the storehouse of the Great Infallibility[50] and laid up in the treasuries of power. It is sanctified above the jewels of explanation; it is beyond what the most subtle of tongues can tell.

Astonishment here is highly prized, and utter poverty essential. Wherefore hath it been said, "Poverty is My pride."[51] And again: "God hath a people beneath the dome of glory, whom

47. Qur'án 6:75.
48. Cf. Qur'án 7:105 etc., and Ḥadíth.
49. The *Mathnaví*.
50. *'Iṣmat-i-Kubrá*, the invariable attribute of the Divine Manifestation.
51. Muḥammad.

He hideth in the clothing of radiant poverty."[52] These are they who see with His eyes, hear with His ears, as it is written in the well-known tradition.

Concerning this realm, there is many a tradition and many a verse, of broad or special relevancy, but two of these will suffice to serve as a light for men of mind and heart.

The first is His statement: "O My Servant! Obey Me and I shall make thee like unto Myself. I say 'Be,' and it is, and thou shalt say 'Be,' and it shall be."

And the second: "O Son of Adam! Seek fellowship with none until thou hast found Me, and whenever thou shalt long for Me, thou shalt find Me close to thee."

Whatever high proofs and wondrous allusions are recounted herein, concern but a single Letter, a single Point. "Such hath been the way of God . . . and no change canst thou find in the way of God."[53]

I began this epistle some time ago, in thy remembrance, and since thy letter had not reached me then, I began with some words of reproach. Now, thy new missive hath dispelled that feeling and causeth Me to write thee. To

52. Ḥadíth.
53. Qur'án 33:62; 48:23.

63

speak of My love for thine Eminence is need-
less. "God is a sufficient witness!"[54] For his
Eminence Shaykh Muḥammad—May God the
Exalted bless him!—I shall confine Myself to
the two following verses which I request be
delivered to him:

> I seek thy nearness, dearer than sweet
> Heaven;
> I see thy visage, fairer than Paradise
> bowers.[55]

When I entrusted this message of love to
My pen, it refused the burden, and it swooned
away. Then coming to itself, it spoke and said,
"Glory be to Thee! To Thee do I turn in peni-
tence, and I am the first of them that believe."[56] Praise be to God, the Lord of the
worlds!

> Let us tell, some other day
> This parting hurt and woe;
> Let us write, some other way,
> Love's secrets—better so.

54. Qur'án 4:164.   55. Sa'dí.   56. Qur'án 7:140.
57. Shams-i-Tabríz, the Ṣúfí who exerted a powerful
influence on Jalálu'd-Dín Rúmí, diverting his attention
from science to Mysticism. A great part of Rúmí's works
are dedicated to him. These lines are from the *Mathnaví*.

64

Leave blood and noise and all of these,
And say no more of <u>Sh</u>ams-i-Tabríz.[57]

Peace be upon thee, and upon those who circle around thee and attain thy meeting.

What I had written ere this hath been eaten by the flies, so sweet was the ink. As Sa'dí saith: "I shall forbear from writing any longer, for my sweet words have drawn the flies about me."

And now the hand can write no more, and pleadeth that this is enough. Wherefore do I say, "Far be the glory of thy Lord, the Lord of all greatness, from what they affirm of Him."[58]

58. Qur'án 37:180.
